The Story Toolkit

Your Step-by-Step Guide to Stories That Sell

Susan Bischoff
Foreword by Kait Nolan

The Story Toolkit

Written and published by Susan Bischoff
Copyright © 2016 Susan Bischoff

All rights reserved. This book or any portion thereofmay not be reproduced or used in any manner whatsoeverwithout the express written permission of the publisherexcept for the use of brief quotations in a book review.

ISBN-13: 978-1539346968
ISBN-10: 153934696X

License Notes

This ebook is licensed for your personal enjoyment and education only. The ebook may not be re-sold or given away to other people. If you would like to share this book with another person, please purchase an additional copy for each person you share it with. If you're reading this book and did not purchase it, or it was not purchased for your use only, then you should purchase your own copy. Thank you for respecting the hard work of this author.

Cover design by Kait Nolan

Contents

Foreword

"I will never be a plotter!" I'm reasonably sure I uttered this statement in precisely the same tone as I once said, "You can pry my dead tree books from my cold, dead hands." Susan and I were brand new critique partners then, and I'm sure I taxed her patience with all my romantic analogies about pantsing being like picking one of those random roads in Ireland and just driving. But the fact is that pantsing a plot is about as likely to net you a solid book as that random road is to land you in the arms of a sexy, single Irishman in want of a wife. You're a lot more likely to just run out of gas. In the rain. With no clue how to get where you really need to go.

That laughter you hear? That's Susan over there laughing and serving me up a piece of "I told you so" cake.

At least it's chocolate cake.

Suffice it to say, this reformed pantser now has a deep, personal relationship with her ereader.

Why the switch? Well, it was a matter of desperation. During my final year of graduate school, I finally admitted that a PhD wasn't going to make me happy. Absolutely the only career that would ever do that was writing, which meant I had to start taking my craft seriously and treating writing as a job. That was a lot easier before I graduated and wound up juggling *three* jobs for nearly a decade, while I put my husband through school. With all that on my plate, I simply did not have the time to spend writing draft after draft on the same book. So my first forays into the world of plotting were borne out of a desire for efficiency. I had little time to write, so that time had to really count.

I tried all kinds of plotting systems. I read books. I read blogs. Susan and I brainstormed endlessly, trying to figure out the right combination of things we needed to know to get from *Once Upon A Time* to *The End*. As we tend to come at plot from entirely opposite sides, this often resulted in a mish-mash of lists that got at *some* of what we were looking for, but not all. We read about goal, motivation, and conflict. We talked about inner wounds. We hypothesized about black moments and the hero's journey. But absolutely nothing really gelled until we stumbled across the concept of story structure. And suddenly, everything we'd been reading coalesced into something that actually made sense. Like finally dialing in an old school transistor radio to the right station.

As I came to realize, plotting is not about creating a road map and figuring out every last thing that happens to your characters before you begin. It's more like building a house. You need to build the proper foundation if the project is to be stable in the end. In the same way that houses have four walls and a roof, all salable stories have a specific underlying structure. You need to know which are the load bearing walls and exactly what purpose they serve in the narrative.

The Story Toolkit evolved from years of refining our understanding of these concepts. And when I say refining, I mean I asked the same questions over-and-over and she kept finding new ways to explain the concepts until I actually understood them. We read more craft books, integrated more concepts. And the end result was a handy-dandy crit partner in my pocket, asking me all the questions that she, as developmental editor extraordinaire, would be asking me anyway. It walked me through the full creation of a plot, from beginning to end, with plenty of explanations and hand holding as I crossed the street from pantser to plotter.

I've never looked back. I fill this puppy out for every single book, and it's made an enormous difference in my ability to get the plot right the *first* time. The only book I've had to write an outright second draft on since the Toolkit's creation is one I didn't use the Toolkit for. Lesson learned.

The Story Toolkit may not be the last plotting book you'll ever need, but it's sure to become an essential part of your arsenal.

Happy writing!

~Kait Nolan

Introduction

It seems like any book on the writing craft should probably start with a reminder that writing is art, and there is no One Right Way of doing things. There are no Toolkit Secret Police. No one is going to check your work and make sure you're doing it "right." If something doesn't work for you, feel free to tweak it, change it, or throw it the hell out. This is about getting your work done, not getting it done my way. Okay?

So, that said...Welcome! And thanks for giving this a try. You're probably here because you're looking for a tool to help you plan your stories. I'm going to assume you're on board with the notion of doing at least some pre-planning and outlining of your work before you jump into writing, so I'm not going to spend the next three pages trying to sell you on the merits of plotting over pantsing (planning your work vs. just jumping in and writing by the seat of your pants).

Elements of the Toolkit have come from a lot of places. I've learned things from so many great minds, and you might hear a lot of things that sound familiar. I've gathered ideas from Larry Brooks, Debra Dixon, Randy Ingermanson, Michael Hauge, James Scott Bell, Dwight Swain, and many others. All these people are brilliant, and worth your study.

Before we jump into the first exercise, I just want to give you a *little* insight about how the Toolkit came into being, how I think about it, so you have a sense of what to expect and where we're going.

Why I Put This Together

The Toolkit is a series of worksheets I made to guide myself from an initial idea through the process of writing a scene-by-scene outline.

I am blessed to have a long-term critique partner. Kait Nolan and I have been exchanging writing and writing ideas for years. I noticed that my brainstorming sessions are a lot more effective when I have Kait there to ask the right questions and direct my thinking. But what about when Kait's not available to be the other half of my brain? I wanted something I could use to ask me those questions.

It's partly that I'm easily overwhelmed. Sometimes you just know what you're going to write about. But sometimes you just have So Many Ideas. I have to pare down from *Everything I Could Possibly Write About,* to *What I Am Going To Write About*. The directing process of this tool helps me do that. It tells me to make my choices. (Which are not set in stone, so don't get antsy. But you have start somewhere, right?)

Since I'm easily overwhelmed, it also helps me to break down the task of planning a novel. Because a novel is huge. And often, great novels have layers of complexity. My brain, which also has to function in other areas of my life, can't hold all this stuff at one time. I need to write it down, and I need an organized way to see it. And, so I don't run screaming, I need a way to break it down into bite-sized pieces.

How It Works

We'll start with Initial Concept, looking at your idea, that initial spark that makes you say, "I want to write a story about…" Sometimes that idea hits you, practically fully formed. Sometimes not. If it's a not, that's okay. It'll get there.

After we get your Initial Concept down, we're going to be looking at things like character, character arc, world building, your antagonist and main conflict, and we'll also look at building a romance in the story, if that's something you do. And we'll be nailing down the main points of your story structure. Don't be afraid to go out of order here. To visit and revisit worksheets as things occur to you. Often, ideas and refinements in one area are going to spark ideas in another. That's just how it works, and it's good. A lot of decision-making is going to take place in this stage. By filling out the worksheets and keeping them all in one place, you'll have gone a long way to making yourself a story or series bible—a reference document to which you can refer back during the writing process, to keep your details straight.

Once you've got all those decisions made, you're going to have a really good sense of the story you're writing. You'll know that you have a complete story with a solid structure. If a formal outline scares you, you don't have to write it. Just take what you now know and discover the rest of your story through writing it.

If you're ready to embrace the outline, there is a series of four beatsheets that will practically do it for you.

CHAPTER 1: PRELIMINARIES

Starting the Toolkit

The rest of this book is going to take you through the worksheets and explain the process, but where you work the sheets in your own practice is up to you. Later in the book, you will find blank worksheets to photocopy, which you can fill out and keep in a binder. You can download a free copy of these worksheets as a PDF file at: http://storytoolkit.com/toolkit-ebook-landing-page/ . I do all my planning, and save all my ideas, in Evernote. I absolutely adore Evernote, and it's where I do my best thinking. You can get started with Evernote for free at: https://goo.gl/dVK6mG.

Now let's move on to the process. I'm a listmaker. I like to do things and check them off or cross them out. So one of the things I like about starting a project is seeing that fresh checklist, with all the blank worksheets, waiting to be completed and crossed off. If planning and scheduling make you happy, this also shows you a breakdown you can put on your calendar. The following is a list of all the worksheets for your novel to-do list.

Novel Checklist

Initial Concept
Worldbuilding
Antagonist, Main Conflict, and Stakes
Major Plot Points
Character: Protagonist
Character: Antagonist
Character: Supporting
Character Arc
Romance Arc
Subplot
Event Brainstorm 1
Event Brainstorm 2
Locations
Act 1 Beat Sheet
Act 2 Beat Sheet
Act 3 Beat Sheet
Act 4 Beat Sheet
Timeline
Proposed Scene List
Finished Scene List
Cast List
Location List
….and any special lists you may add, links to research, etc.

1. Initial Concept

- What is the beginning concept or inspiration for this story?
- What do you know about the main characters? List some wants/needs and fears.
- What do you know about the story world?
- What do you know about the story problem? What is the main character's goal, motivation, and conflict?
- What do you know about the antagonist?

Explanation

Planning the building of a novel is a process of both drilling down and building up. We need to start weeding out the possibilities to find a definite direction for our story, and we also need to build up the direction and elements we choose.

What is the beginning concept or inspiration for this story?

This is just what it appears to be. Write anything here, whether it's just a few lines or several paragraphs. Often, just the act of writing your ideas down helps your brain start the refining process.

What do you know about the main characters? List some wants/needs and fears.

You don't have to write a character sketch here, but often you'll know at least something about the character(s). Try to push a little further and ask yourself, what does this character want and need? Wants and needs lead to character motivation. We definitely want to know the character's motivation, so get your brain thinking on that.

Wants, needs, and fears also play into stakes. What's at stake for your character when he goes after the story goal? What does she stand to gain if she gets it? What does he stand to lose if he fails? What does she fear might happen if she doesn't win in the end? What does he fear might happen if he tries to go after this thing?

What do you know about the story world?

By "story world," I basically mean the setting. But I don't like the word "setting." It sounds like a movie set. A fake room with furniture and other props your characters are going to move around in. Or it sounds like it's going to lead you to tell me something like "present day New Orleans."

Which is so not enough.

I love the word Larry Brooks used for this. *Arena.* Feel how encompassing that is. Setting matters. Or it should. Even if your story takes place in a bar, or in a small town, even if it's something that seems universally understood and familiar, with no faster-than-light spaceships, vampires, robots, or wizards.

We tend to think that world building really only matters in genres like science fiction and fantasy. I don't think it's so much that it matters more. Maybe it's just more work to build those worlds up from scratch.

When you think about story world, you also want to think about the rules of the society your characters are living in. If you're a period romance junkie, you've seen how those rules affect *everything*, from the characters' goals and motivation, to what they can get away with, to how they respond to any given situation.

In a spaceship, you might know that you have limited resources, that you're dependent on your life support system, that people's actions are dictated by a strict set of rules meant to ensure safety and survival. The spaceship isn't just a backdrop. Being in it affects how the characters respond to the problems you throw at them.

But how does that work in a contemporary setting? If my world is "present day, New York City," well, everyone knows New York, New York. But there are so many different New Yorks. I'm not even talking about a secret world under the subways. I mean, imagine your story takes place primarily in an office tower. Your characters are in the business world. The business world has its own set of rules that affects what they're going to do. How they act, how they dress, how they speak, what their goals are…

Now imagine your story takes place on the street, in a ghetto, and your characters are gang members. They live by another set of rules.

The business world, gang land, high society, mob families, ethnic enclaves… these are all microcosms within present day New York City that will have their own rules.

Also, the setting is often the source of conflicts for your characters. Take any hospital drama, for example. Or the Hellmouth that Sunnydale was located on in *Buffy the Vampire Slayer.* A law office brings legal cases and clients. A police station brings your characters into contact with cases, criminals, victims, and witness. The setting may not be the source of your character's story goal and main conflict, but it can be an obstacle generating machine to ensure nothing goes smoothly for the people in your story.

What do you know about the story problem? What is the main character's goal, motivation, and conflict?

When I say "story problem," I mean goal. What is your character after? And please, have a goal. No one picking up commercial fiction wants to read a story about a directionless character, wandering aimlessly. Solve a problem, win a prize, escape something…

A CHARACTER goes after a GOAL, because of a MOTIVATION, but an ANTAGONIST causes CONFLICT.

Substitute your details into that sentence, and you have a premise.

Andi, a girl from the wrong side of the tracks, wants to date Blaine, a boy from a wealthy family, because he's cute and she feels like there's something between them, but Blaine's friend Steph, and other "richies," make things hard for the couple. [Pretty in Pink]

You know there's more to it—that pitch doesn't even mention Duckie, but that's the basic story in a nutshell.

Sarah Connor, an ordinary waitress, just wants to stay alive [motivation apparent], but a cyborg called a Terminator has been sent from the future to assassinate her before she can give birth to mankind's future savior. [The Terminator]

Robbie, a wedding singer, wants to win the heart of Julia, the new waitress who is beautiful, funny, sweet, and completely captivating, but she's engaged to jerkweed, Glenn, who can offer Julia the kind of financial security that Robbie doesn't have. [The Wedding Singer]

You get the idea. Once you start refining your story problem, the character's motivation to solve it, and the kinds of conflicts he is going to face, it becomes easier to craft a premise. In just a little bit, I want to talk more about ideas, concepts, and premises, and why honing down to a premise is important. But first, let's finish up this section.

What do you know about the antagonist?

Your antagonist is the person, group, or force that brings about the main conflict in your story. It can be a proper villain, a rival, the other team, a government, or even a natural disaster. You don't have to know much right now, but give some thought to who would be behind the conflict you envision for your story, and start writing down some ideas.

Idea, Concept, Premise

Before we move on to the next worksheet, I want to talk about this notion of idea vs. concept vs. premise.

In the last exercise, we were doing two things. 1) We were brainstorming ideas for our story, and trying to push our brains a little further into the directions we need to go, in order to nail down some details for our story. 2) We were trying to drill down from a vague idea to specific premise.

Understanding the how of going from idea to concept to premise is a great exercise in itself, because it can help steer you toward getting the most effective stories out of your ideas.

An idea is often very general. It's often, in fact, much more general than we realize when we first think of it. If you've ever had that thing where you think you have a brilliant idea, and then you start telling it to a friend, and they start asking questions, and you suddenly realize you've got a whole lotta nothin'—well, you probably know what I'm saying. An idea is great, but it's not really a story yet.

I'm going to write a story about the zombie apocalypse.

Great idea! I love that! But a story about the zombie apocalypse could turn out to be *The Walking Dead, 28 Days Later, World War Z,* or a host of other things. All "zombie apocalypse" gets you is "it's gonna have zombies" and "things will be bad."

So you need to move that idea along to the concept phase, in which you start to pick some elements that are going to make the story what it is. These are the key things you want to write about.

I'm going to write about the zombie apocalypse, but instead of focusing solely on the humans fighting the zombies, I'm going to show the humans' struggle to survive after the modern world is gone, to find food, safety, medical supplies. I'm going to focus on people. What will a person become when faced with that environment? I'm going to show the dark side, the man's inhumanity to man stuff, but also the show people growing in character, forming new family units…

Okay, so you're writing *The Walking Dead,* or something close to it. But it's still not a tellable tale. Note the absence of story elements: characters, specific goals and motivations, and specific conflicts. Once you make up some of those things, you can start crafting premises for the stories you're going to tell in the series. Like the one for the first TV episode:

Rick Grimes, a small-town sheriff's deputy who has just awakened from a coma, leaves the hospital and goes into the deserted town in search of his family, but encounters dead people who want to eat him.

(Much like a goal of survival, a search for something like family is a universally understood motivation.)

Let's try one more.

Idea: *I want to write a story in which terrorists create a hostage situation, and one guy, working alone, saves the day.*

Concept: *Terrorists take over an office building. This one guy, an off-duty cop, totally unprepared, takes them out one by one. He's not prepared, and no one can bring him anything, so he can only use things found in an office building, and things he steals from the bad guys. The bad guys are not really in it for the politics, they're actually thieves.*

Premise: *John McClane, a New York City cop, travels to LA to spend the holidays with his estranged family and try to work things out with his wife, Holly. But when terrorists take over the building where she works, making hostages of Holly and her coworkers, John is the only one who can save them. Without preparation or backup, he uses anything at his disposal to eliminate the bad guys, foil their plot to steal millions of dollars in bearer bonds, and stop them from killing the hostages to make their getaway. [Die Hard]*

Idea: That spark of "I want to write about…"

Concept: Start throwing in specific elements you want to use to make the story yours.

Premise: Come up with the characters, goals, motivation, antagonist, and conflicts that will work with your chosen elements to tell a story.

CHAPTER 2: SETTING YOUR STORY

The Importance of Setting

When we talked about worldbuilding in the last chapter, we talked about the importance of setting, and what it brings to the story. Let's get a little more into that.

There are some genres that rely heavily on setting. Three that come to mind are science fiction, fantasy, and historical. In all of these, the setting is a big part of why the reader shows up, in order to be taken to places with futuristic technology, magic, or the romance of a bygone era. To these types of stories, worldbuilding is absolutely critical.

But stories which take place in our world, in our time, have just as much power of transportation. Think of setting, not as a place, but as a microcosm.

I mentioned period romance as an example earlier. What makes a period drama? We've got the costumes, the sets, the old-fashioned speech, and manners. The manners! Everything is determined by the society of the day. The characters must adhere to their rigid class structure, or else. The conflicts in a period drama often arise when the demands of society clash with the needs or desires of the characters. In that way, the story world becomes completely enmeshed with the plot.

But look at all the cultures we have today.

We have a corporate culture with its own set of rules and mores. It lends itself to stories about characters striving to succeed, or to hold onto their personal beliefs in a driven, success-oriented culture that is often portrayed as greedy or downright evil.

We have small town culture. Small towns can be warm, welcoming places where everyone helps their neighbor. Or they can be closed, unwelcoming, and full of people who are suspicious of outsiders. Either way, people know each other, gossip runs rampant, and everyone knows your business. A bad place to have secrets!

There are stories about street gangs, motorcycle clubs, sports teams, the military, law enforcement agencies, students in high school, boarding school, college… all of these groups have their own rules, and lend themselves to stories where those rules clash with the characters. There may be stories in which the characters strive to improve their lot within the group, or possibly to leave the group. There may be stories where a character has been ejected from their familiar culture and has to find their place in a new one.

Star Trek taught us that, underneath the latex that makes people look like they're from another world, we're all still people. Often setting is not so much the world you visit, but the people who make the world what it is.

Think about that as you go forward and plan the events of your story.

2. Worldbuilding

A lot of this is for inspiration purposes. Do not feel that you need to answer all the questions. Don't force what's not relevant.

When?

- Time period- (Current day, historic period, future, alternate reality…)
  - Jot down some things you know about the time period in which your story takes place and how that will affect the story and/or characters.
- Season-
  - How does the season affect the story? Holidays?
- Weather conditions that affect the story?

Where?

- Where does your story take place? (Town, country, planet, school…)
- Jot down a general idea of how the world itself will affect the story and its characters.
- Geography
  - Any mountains, bodies of water, roads, lack of roads, borders, flora, fauna, etc., that will affect the story

Who?

- Are there specific groups of people in your world that will influence the story?
  - Ethnic cultures
  - Cliques or organizations
  - Powerful families or clans
  - Societal rules or norms, culture

What?

- **Politics?**
  - Are there details about the government or political situation that affect the story?
  - Are there economic details that affect the story?
  - Is there or has there been a war that affects the story?
- **Technology?**
- **History?**
  - Regional history, ethnic heritage

Explanation

This is really basic, generic worldbuilding stuff. If you have something more suitable to your particular genre, use it, by all means.

There was much debate in my mind, about whether to put this close to the beginning, or close to the end. I finally decided to put it close to the beginning because I think that, even in contemporary, real world stories, setting is and should be integral to the plot.

On the other hand, ***don't get carried away.***

Don't build more setting than you need at this time. Write down what comes to you now, at this stage. Later on, when you know a lot more about what happens in the story, we'll come back to the idea of setting to work on specific locations.

As you can see, I've organized the brainstorming by question words.

When- It's not so important that you answer all the questions about when the story takes place. It's more important to think about *how the when affects the story.*

Where- Don't think just about what the place names are, and what geographical features might exist. Think about how those features will affect the characters and story. Think about how those features might shape the people who live in that where and how that adds to the story.

Who- Who can get interesting, because the whos can bring the conflict. If not the main conflict, then they can definitely supply other obstacles for your character. They can also provide help. What kinds of people inhabit your story world, and how can they work for or against your protagonist? Remember that society, and the rules it imposes, represent a huge component of the story world, so give that some thought now.

What- Politics, technology, and history might play a role in your story. They might also play a role in shaping the culture that inhabits your story world.

Think about the interplay here. Does geography affect politics? Does technology affect culture? Is there a group that became powerful because of something that happened in the history of the place?

CHAPTER 3: ESTABLISHING CONFLICT

Bad Guys and the Problems They Cause

There is no drama, no real story, without conflict. Without something to struggle against, you have something more like an anecdote. So you must, must, must have something that lies between your characters and attaining their goal. Otherwise they're just marking time until the end when they reach the goal, and the whole thing reads like filler.

Before you can move on, you'll need to make at least some headway in nailing down what your main conflict is going to be, and who (or what) is going to bring that to your good guys.

In some respects, an antagonist is just another character, and all notions about making good characters apply. But, as the agent of conflict, the antagonist isn't just *any* character. Because your antagonist is so critical to your story, he deserves some special attention.

Since a good villain should never appear formulaic or stereotypical, it's hard to come up with a method of "this is how you do it"— especially when we're talking about different genres. What we need is a framework in which to think about the Conflict your main character(s) will face, and who will be the Agent of that conflict.

3. Antagonist, Main Conflict, and Stakes

Part 1

- Conflict or Villain? Where do you start?
    - You start where you're inspired to start. Write whatever you can about either the conflict or the villain in your story.

Part 2

- If you wrote about the conflict, write about the antagonist who would confront your character(s) with it.
- If you wrote about a villain, write down a problem he could cause for your hero.

Part 3

Let's take our thinking a little deeper...

- What is your protagonist's weakness?
- Why is your antagonist the one perfect agent to exploit that weakness and force the protagonist to overcome it?
- In what way(s) are your protagonist and antagonist alike?

Part 4

Let's talk stakes. Consequences.

Assumption: at the end of the novel, your protagonist solves the story problem. Protagonist "wins," antagonist "loses."

- What does your protagonist gain by solving the story problem and being the winner?
- If your antagonist were to win at the end of the story, what would he gain?
- What does your antagonist lose at the end of the story?
- If your protagonist were to fail, what would he lose?

Explanation

Part 1

- Conflict or Villain? Where do you start?
    - You start where you're inspired to start. With the part that made you want to write this story.

Maybe your story came out of wanting to show something about a change in a person or relationship, and conflicts and villains weren't included in the package. In that case, think about what kind of experience could inspire that change. Is it struggling against a particular person? That person is your villain. Write about him. Is it an experience like a journey or tackling a problem? The reason for the journey, or the problem to be solved, is the conflict. Write about that.

Part 2

- If you wrote about the conflict, write about the antagonist who would confront your character(s) with it.
- If you wrote about a villain, write down a problem he could cause for your hero.

For brainstorming purposes, it might help to think in terms of how your antagonist relates to your protagonist. Is the antagonist a gatekeeper, a rival, an evil fiend, an authority figure, someone with a grudge?

The antagonist might keep the protagonist from the thing she wants most (a kidnapped child, the throne, the medicine, freedom, chocolate).

The antagonist and the protagonist might be in competition for the same thing (a magic element, head cheerleader, a job, the cutest boy).

The antagonist might want to bring about a situation the protagonist doesn't want to see happen (the end of the world, the end of the protagonist's marriage, family business demolished for parking garage, the protagonist's death).

Part 3

- Let's take our thinking a little deeper...
- What is your protagonist's weakness?
- Why is your antagonist the one perfect agent to exploit that weakness and force the protagonist to overcome it?
- In what way(s) are your protagonist and antagonist alike?

Working through this section can help you write a Character Arc for your protagonist—something which readers find very satisfying. If nothing else, it may help you get ideas for things your antagonist will do to make life difficult for your protagonist.

Your protagonist has a weakness (Goodness, I hope so. Please, tell me your character's not perfect.)During the course of the story, your protagonist may need to overcome that weakness in order to overcome the conflict presented by the antagonist. Think about how that weakness, or character flaw, will make it harder for your protagonist to reach his goals. (This is fodder for a good character arc.)

You might also think of the weakness as a "skewed view of the world," something the protagonist thinks about how the world works, which is not necessarily true. In order for him to achieve his story goals, he'll have to learn a lesson that will change his outlook. Why is your antagonist so perfect for helping him learn the lesson?

The last question is an interesting one to contemplate. Think about your own feelings when you realize that a protagonist and antagonist are really two sides of the same coin. Neat, right? You already know they're different, because one's the good guy and one's the bad guy. But thinking about how they're the same can enrich your depiction of your antagonist. It may make your hero a little darker, but it will probably also make your villain more human. Both characters will benefit from the process.

Part 4

Let's talk stakes. Consequences.

Assumption: at the end of the novel, your protagonist solves the story problem. Protagonist "wins," antagonist "loses."

- What does your protagonist gain by solving the story problem and being the winner?
- If your antagonist were to win at the end of the story, what would s/he gain?
- What does your antagonist lose at the end of the story?
- If your protagonist were to fail, what would he lose?

Stakes are important because they provide character motivation. Both your protagonist and antagonist must be motivated, they must care about what they're doing. They must have reasons for their actions, rather than performing random actions that lead the reader to the thing about the story that made you want to write it.

Stakes also give the reader a reason to care. If your protagonist is striving to gain something, the reader can want that for him and root for him to get it. If your protagonist will lose something, or be punished for failure to solve the story problem, it can create a sense of urgency and suspense for your reader. Will he make it??

Stakes add weight and importance, as well as motivation.

CHAPTER 4: BUILDING THE STORY SKELETON

Getting Into Story Structure

In the next worksheet, we'll gather up the things we've figured out so far, and, along with some understanding of story structure, we'll start plotting out some of the major events of the story. At the end of it, we're going to have a bare bones outline of something that really looks like a story!

I'm not going to write pages to convince you why you should follow this story structure notion. I figure you're already looking for some help with this plotting thing, and this helps. Trust me, it helps so much.

There are whole books devoted to story structure, and my go-to guy for this is Larry Brooks. If you're new to the concepts here, or if you need to deepen your understanding, try his STORY ENGINEERING.

4. Major Plot Points

Story = A CHARACTER pursues a GOAL because of MOTIVATION, but is hampered by CONFLICT.

Character
Who is your protagonist?
Goal
What is the ultimate end goal for your protagonist?
Motivation
Why is your protagonist in pursuit of his goal?
Conflict
What is the antagonist (or antagonistic force) that stands between your protagonist and his goal?
How/why does the antagonist attempt to prevent the protagonist from attaining or achieving his goal?

To chart the course of a journey, one must know one's destination.
In a story, we like to call that
The End.

Climax

- What do you know about the climax of the story?
- How does the ending deliver a knock-out experience?
- How does the ending solve the story problem?
- How is the protagonist the catalyst for solving the story problem?

No one shows up at the deli and says,
"Give me anything on rye."
What's in the middle is pretty important.

In creating a character motivated toward a goal, great strides were made toward having an Act 1.

In creating an antagonist and knocking it down, great strides were made toward having an Act 4.

Knowing how story structure works will help you fill in the middle.

Brainstorm for ideas about the major events of your story. It's okay to be vague on what you don't know, but write something, even if it's just a reminder of what needs to happen functionally at that point in the story. Remember, this isn't an outline, we're still just brainstorming.

Act 1
II-
FPP-

Act 2
PP1-
MP-

Act 3
PP2-
SPP-

Act 4
KO-
END-

Explanation

Story = A CHARACTER pursues a GOAL because of MOTIVATION, but is hampered by CONFLICT.

Character
Who is your protagonist?
Goal
What is the ultimate end goal for your protagonist?
Motivation
Why is your protagonist in pursuit of his goal?
Conflict
What is the antagonist (or antagonistic force) that stands between your protagonist and his goal?

How/why does the antagonist attempt to prevent the protagonist from attaining or achieving his goal?

GMC: GOAL, MOTIVATION, AND CONFLICT is an excellent book by Debra Dixon. It's largely about the importance of character motivation, and how it drives the story.

These are your essential starting elements. By now you should have some good ideas for answering the questions above.

One thing to note is that, after finishing this section, you should be better able to answer the question "What's your story about?" without telling that person everything you've come up with so far. Knowing these core elements can help you be more concise about explaining the heart of your story. Return here when it's time to write your pitch, your blurb, or any time you feel off track.

Climax

- What do you know about the climax of the story?
- How does the ending deliver a knock-out experience?
- How does the ending solve the story problem?
- How is(are) the main character(s) the catalyst for solving the story problem?

James Scott Bell talks about **LOCK** in his book PLOT & STRUCTURE. It's yet another way to think about collecting the key elements of your story. **LOCK** stand for **L**ead, **O**bjective, **C**onflict, and **K**nock-out.

At this stage, it's easy to say, "And there's a big fight and the good guy wins, and the bad guy runs away."

I cannot urge you strongly enough to give it a little more thought. So many books stall in the middle because the writer has only the vaguest notion of where they're going. It might *seem* like you know the end, but if you can't write down any specifics right now, you probably don't know as much as you think you do.

Remember, nothing you do here is written in stone. These are your notes and no one is going to see them. You are *always* free to change your mind, to make whatever changes you need along the way. So try to give yourself a little help by way of a destination. When you know where you're going, your set-up throughout the rest of the story may be richer for it.

What is this "knock-out experience"? Well, it really means to suggest that you craft an ending that will have some kind of punch for the reader. That may be a literal punch, in which the protagonist smacks the crap out of the antagonist. Or it may be more of an emotional punch, as the hero, stripped bare of his emotional armor, finally wins the heart of the woman he loves. The idea here is to say, "This ending is really going to resonate with the reader because, during the story, I'm going to…"

How does the ending solve the story problem? It may seem obvious to you that the ending *should* solve the story problem. But we've all read that unfortunate story in which all the action seems to be leading up to one thing, and the ending is actually about something else. Let's not do that. Be clear, right from the beginning, that your story problem will get solved and how your ending shows that happening.

Finally, how is the protagonist the catalyst for solving the story problem? Again, might seem obvious, but you'd be surprised. No you wouldn't. We all know that the phrase *deus ex machina* exists for a reason. The reader has been following your protagonist on his journey to solving the story problem and wants to see the protagonist succeed. No gimmies here. Make sure your ending satisfies.

Crash Course on Story Structure

The beginning of your story is a setup. At the end, everything comes to fruition. The middle part is the building. The buildup of events that lead to the climax, the buildup of experiences that result in character growth. It's the longest part of the book and the hardest for most writers to tackle. Kait likes to call it The Valley of the Shadow of the Middle.

Often at least part of what makes it hard, is that many writers go in with a solid notion of how the story starts, a pretty good idea how it ends, and a few scraps of inspiration to throw at the middle. No wonder it's hard!

The thing that most helped me learn to muddle through the middle was learning story structure. Below is a list of the main plot points, where they land in each quarter of the story, and how they function in a novel.

Act 1

Inciting Incident (II)

- This confusing little gem of a plot point *can* happen anywhere in Act 1, including the opening scene.
- Could also function as the **FPP** (in which case it would have to come at the end of Act 1).
- The moment that introduces the story problem (goal).It doesn't necessarily present a decision point for the protagonist; it may just hint at the decision point to come.
- It may suggest a possible solution.
- It plants the seed that will soon blossom into the FPP.

First Plot Point (FPP)

- The last scene of Act 1.
- It sets the character on the path to the goal.
- It pushes the character through a door from the world they know into the story world.
- The stakes, the things the character has to win or lose, create a choice for the character about whether or not to pursue this goal, and demand a decision.
- It introduces the antagonist or reveals something new about the true nature of the antagonist.

Act 2

Pinch Point 1 (PP1)

- Falls at the middle of Act 2
- The main character faces down their first real challenge
- It's a reminder of the existence of the antagonist
- Shows the character is woefully unprepared to achieve the goal

Midpoint (MP)

- This scene or sequence of scenes happens at the approximate midpoint of the story.
- It turns the story on its ear in some way.
- It changes the context of the story. From this point on, it's a whole new ball game, everything is seen in a different light, etc.
- It changes the character from "wanderer" to "warrior," from a reactive character to a proactive character.
- The point at which a "ticking clock" often starts
- Is sometimes a false victory- something the character tried for and won, which turned out to be a set-back in terms of achieving the goal.

- Is sometimes a false defeat- something the character tried for and lost, but learned something or discovered that it actually better positioned them to attain their goal.

Act 3
Pinch Point 2 (PP2)

- Falls at the middle of Act 3.
- Now proactive, the main character probably seeks out this challenge.
- The main character is harshly defeated.
- It's another reminder of the antagonist.
- It often creates an "all is lost," or hopeless feeling in the character.

Second Plot Point (SPP)

- The last scene of Act 3
- Something new is discovered by or revealed to the character
- This new information is the last piece of the puzzle, or in some way gives them a new means to go after the antagonist and the goal.
- It creates a renewed sense of hope and drive in the character.
- It sends them into Act 4.

Act 4
Climax (KO)

- The "knock-out" defeat of the antagonist
- The WIN
- MUST be a direct result of the actions of the main character

Denouement (END)

- The wind-down after the climax
- The final scene
- Loose ends are tied up
- Explanations are given
- The main character is shown to be a new person
- The character may demonstrate new thoughts or feelings about self or their world
- Rewards, praise, etc, may be received by the main character

I hope you can now see a real story forming, and that you're getting excited about telling it.

CHAPTER 5: GETTING INTO CHARACTER

The Character Worksheets

The most important thing to understand about the character worksheets is that they're not intended to be filled out completely.

If you have *no earthly idea* what your character's favorite time of day is, that's probably not the kind of thing you would put in your story anyway. If you know that it's early evening, maybe it's because that's when she comes home from work, takes off her bra, and turns on Netflix. Since that might tell us something about who your character is, it becomes relevant.

Avoid spending your time and mental energy on that which is irrelevant. The brain doesn't like irrelevancies, and if you come up with a bunch of character information you don't need, there's a fair chance your brain will find a way to write it into the story in such a way that your readers will roll their eyes and wonder why you had to tell that seemingly irrelevant factoid. Readers dislike irrelevancies even more than brains do.

If these character sheets don't thrill you, there are a million more out there. Do character interviews, or journal entries, or whatever you need to do to get a sense of who your characters are.

5. Character: Protagonist

The bulk of this list is for inspiration purposes only. Beyond the basic things you need to write and plot—name, age, and physical description—fill in only those things that jump out at you. Give a moment of consideration to each, but if nothing comes to mind, skip it as either irrelevant to your story or best added on the fly.

Personal Information

- Name/Nickname-
- Tags-
- Age-
- Birthplace-
- Occupation-
- Special talent or skill-
- Living Situation-

Physical Characteristics

- Height and build-
- Hair, eyes, etc.-
- Fashion sense-

Character Arc

- Who is this character meant to be?
- How is that different from who they think they are when the story begins?

Relationships

- List any relevant people and their relationship with, or effect on, the character. Parents, siblings, best friend, worst enemy, boss...

Dear Things

- What does your character really care about?

Personality Style

- Response to change (hates it? seeks it? rolls with it?)-
- Coping methods-
- Best quality-
- Worst flaw-
- What does this character think is the worst thing that could happen to them?

Favorite Things

- Color-
- Music-
- Place (why?)-
- Time of day-
- Holiday or season-
- Food-
- Activity/Hobby-
- Aversions-

Defining Moments

- What is the worst thing that has ever happened to this character?
- What is this character's favorite memory?
- Was there a moment from the past that continues to affect the character today?

Survival and Attitude

- What does the character always carry?
- What does the character always have in the refrigerator (in their living space, etc.)?

Relevant Backstory

- What about this character's past is relevant to the story?

Likability

- Why do you/why will we love this character?

Explanation

I'm just going to go through and talk about some things in here that might raise questions…

Tags- By this I mean things associated with character's looks or habits that you'll mention often, as a signal to the reader that *this* is who I'm talking about. Hair or eye color, facial expression, catch phrases, gestures. This is sometimes useful if you're working with a large cast.

Living situation- Apartment, house, rents, owns, vagabond, lives alone, lives with mother, lives with sibling…

Dear things- The way to make your reader care about your character is to make your character care about something, or someone.

Relevant Backstory- See how I put that "relevant" in there? Really we only ever want to know the parts of the character's past that help us understand the story now. If it doesn't explain why they are where they are, or pertain to where they're going in some way, we probably don't need to know it.

Why do you love this character? Why will we love this character? I think this is an important question to ask yourself about your protagonist because it's good for the reader to like him. It's easier to root for people we can care about. And you don't want your critique partner to ask you, "Why should I care what happens to this guy?" And you're like, "Uhhhh…because I wrote him."

6. Character: Antagonist

The bulk of this list is for inspiration purposes only. Beyond the basic things you need to write and plot—name, age, and physical description—fill in only those things that jump out at you. Give a moment of consideration to each, but if nothing comes to mind, skip it as either irrelevant to your story or best added on the fly.

Personal Information

- Name/Nickname-
- Tags-
- Age-
- Birthplace-
- Occupation-
- Special talent or skill-
- Living Situation-

Physical Characteristics

- Height and build-
- Hair, eyes, etc.-
- Fashion sense-

Character Arc

- Who is this character meant to be?
- How is that different from who they think they are when the story begins?

Relationships

- List any relevant people and their relationship with, or effect on, the character. Parents, siblings, best friend, worst enemy, boss...

Dear Things

- What does your character really care about?

Bad Guy Stuff

- Why is this character at odds with your protagonist?
- Why is this character perfect for exploiting the weakness of your protagonist?
- Is your antagonist genuinely bad or just misunderstood? How did that happen?
- What does this character think about himself?
- Could this character be redeemed?

Personality Style

- Response to change (hates it? seeks it? rolls with it?)-
- Coping methods-
- Best quality-
- Worst flaw-
- What does this character think is the worst thing that could happen to them?

Favorite Things

- Color-
- Music-
- Place (why?)-
- Time of day-
- Holiday or season-
- Food-
- Activity/Hobby-
- Aversions-

Defining Moments

- What is the worst thing that has ever happened to this character?
- What is this character's favorite memory?
- Was there a moment from the past that continues to affect the character today?
- What started your antagonist down the wrong path?

Survival and Attitude

- What does the character always carry?
- What does the character always have in the refrigerator (in their living space, etc.)?

Relevant Backstory

- What about this character's past is relevant to the story?

Reader Response

- Why will we love to hate this character?

Explanation

You'll notice that the Antagonist sheet is nearly identical to the Protagonist sheet, with the addition of some **Bad Guy Stuff** questions.

Any of these things can help you make a more three-dimensional villain, and how much you use really depends on how much your antagonist actually appears in your story, or how much you feel you need to humanize him.

7. Character: Supporting

1. Make one for each character.
2. Keep these simple. Leave these characters open to be what you need them to be, in order tofacilitatethe writing.
3. Include the character name, book title, and series name, and keep it in your bible
4. Come back and add details as you write the story.
5. Thank yourself later.

- **Name**
- **Tags**
- **Age**
- **Physical description**
- **Relationship to/with main character(s)**
- **Style**
- **Occupation/Special skills**
- **Is this character associated with a specific location?**
- **Quirk**
- **Likes**
- **Hates**
- **Fears**
- **Living situation**
- **Family**
- **Relevant backstory**
- **What does the future hold for this character?**

Explanation

The worksheet for supporting characters is a lot shorter. You'll want to sketch in things you know are important, things that will help you power through the writing without spending time figuring out details, but a full workup isn't necessary.

You've got your story skeleton now, so you have your main plot events. What characters does the story need to make those things happen? Start a **cast list** in your story bible, then work a character sheet for each.

Supporting characters are tools to use when you need them. If you've already introduced Jenny as a girly-girl in chapter one—for no other reason than that was something that occurred to you at the time, then when you need a tomboy in chapter three, you'll wind up making up yet another character. Keep the supporting characters vague enough to become what you need.

What is necessary is that you keep track of the details if you have a lot of characters, *especially* if you're writing a series. You might not remember that Katie had green eyes in the first book when you give her brown eyes in the third book, but the latecoming reader, who plows through all three books on the holiday weekend, is bound to notice.

CHAPTER 6: SPINNING THREADS FOR WEAVING

What Are Threads?

Threads is the term I'm using for things other than the main plot which you'll want to follow through the story. I'm going to give you sheets for a Character Arc thread, a Romance Arc thread, and a Subplot thread.

You may not have a subplot or a romance, and you may decide you don't much want to make a fuss over character arc either. But since I've put a lot of story development into the Character Arc sheet, I'd suggest going through it to see if it helps you flesh out the story a little more.

8. Character Arc

In life, we are often trapped in an Identity of who we think we are. In fiction, a character moves from that Identity to the Essence of who he was meant to be.

- What does your character need and lack?
- What lesson does your character need to learn?
- What does your character really care about?
- What are the internal identity issues (inner demons or skewed world view) that keep your character from attaining what they need?
- How does who he thinks he is differ from who he is meant to be?
- What external plot issues will be affected by these identity issues?

What are the major plot points?
II-
FPP-
PP1-
MP-
PP2-
SPP-
FAS-
KO-
End-

Act 1: Intro of the Orphan

Establishes all the set-up points for the story, including what the character wants, needs, and lacks, what the character has to win or lose.

Opening

- What does the character lack or need and how will you show that when you introduce them?

Inciting Incident

- What is the inciting incident? How does it begin to set up for the first plot point?
- How does the inciting incident poke at your character's fears and insecurities?
- How will you show what's at stake, what will be on the table to gain and lose at the first plot point?
- How will you show what aspects of personal identity, who they *think* they are, will get in the way of achieving the goal that will be set at the first plot point?

First Plot Point

- What is the FPP? What goal does it set for the character?
- *External Arc:* What happens at the FPP that will force the character into the story world?
- *Internal Arc:* How will you show that the character is reluctant to move forward but chooses to anyway?

Act 2: The Wanderer sets off

In which the character tries to learn skills and gather resources while coping with an unfamiliar world

Regrouping

- How does the character react immediately following the FPP? What does he decide to do next?

Pinch Point 1

- What is PP1? How does it show that the character doesn't have what it takes to stand up to the antagonistic force and achieve the goal?

Midpoint: The Flip

- What happens at the MP?
- *External:* How does the MP flip the story on its ear and change the context? *Internal:* How does the MP create a flip in terms of turning the Wanderer into a Warrior, reactive to proactive?

Act 3: The Warrior

In which the character goes on the warpath, only to be smacked down

The Doomed Plan

- What is the new plan to go for the goal and why is it doomed? (Hint: it's because of *Identity*—the character's skewed world view or inner demon that causes them to make wrong choices.)

PP2: The Doomstick

- What is the wicked smackdown dealt to the character?
- *External:* How does this make it seem like *all is lost*and attainment of the goal is now impossible?
- *Internal:* How does PP2 show the character's retreat to their*Identity*, and how he is no matchfor the antagonistic force?

Second Plot Point

- What is the SPP and how does it work to push the character into the final Act? What piece of the puzzle does it give the character that he didn't have before?

Act 4: Ultimate Badass Martyr

In which the character fully becomes who he was meant to be, saves the day, wins the prize.

Final Action Sequence

- In the FAS, how will you show the character facing his inner demon/learning his lesson?

Climax

- At the climax, how does the character show that he has learned his lesson and/or become who he was meant to be, and how does that allow him to finally achieve a Knock Out against the antagonistic force?

Denouement

- At the End, how will you show the character has become who he was meant to be?

What is the theme of your story?

Explanation

The terms Identity and Essence come from Michael Hague, author of WRITING SCREENPLAYS THAT SELL.

The heart of character arc is the change in a character from the beginning of the story to the end of the story, which takes place *as a result of the story experience.*

The Character Arc is sometimes called the Internal Arc, while the main plot of the story is the External Arc. Debra Dixon also talks about the Internal Arc vs. The External Arc in GMC, which I referenced earlier.

The idea here is that you have your main plot, the thing where the protagonist is out to solve a story problem, for a good reason, but is hampered by an antagonist. That problem is *outside* your character. External.

Then you have your character arc, the story wherein your hero (learns his lesson and) changes from beginning to end. This change takes place *inside* your character. Internal.

And, in order for everything to feel all integrated and brilliant, it's nice when your character needs to learn the lesson and have that change happen, *in order to solve the story problem.*

- What does your character need and lack?
- What lesson do they need to learn?

These are about the character arc. You might find some clues in the work you did earlier on motivation. You don't require a need, a lack, *and* a lesson. Some characters don't really learn a lesson, per se, they just grow into a new person.

- What does your character really care about?

You might look back to your Conflict sheet and the work you did on stakes for this. Readers really respond to a character who cares about *something.* It gives the readers something to root for, to want for the character, and draws them into the story.

- What are the internal identity issues (inner demons or skewed world view) that keep your character from attaining what he needs?
- How does who he thinks he is differ from who he was meant to be?

I put this on the character sheet earlier, so you could start thinking about it. By "identity" we're really asking, "how does he see himself?"

What's important here is to think about how this character's personality problems affect his inner life.

Ex. Maybe he needs companionship, but he identifies as a loner so he drives everyone away. By the end of the story he will learn to be part of a team.

- What external plot issues will be affected by these identity issues?

This is asking how his inner garbage is going to affect his ability to solve the story problem.

Ex. The protagonist keeps failing to solve the problem because he's trying to do everything alone. Only by learning to work with the team can he achieve his goals. (And, in doing that, he gets the companionship he so desperately needed.)

Major Plot Points

This section asks for the major plot points, which you brainstormed on the Major Plot Points worksheet. There are a few reasons for this:

To get them on the page where you're working

To refresh your memory

To see if you get any new ideas or insights by rewriting them

So definitely rewrite them, as opposed to copy/pasting.

Elaborating and tying in

The next section takes you through all of your major plot points, one by one. As you work through, you'll have space to expand on any ideas you have about what happens. Since you know so much more about your characters now, and since things have been incubating nicely as you've been taking time to work on this, you might find you have a lot of spontaneous insights.

The other thing you're doing in this section is mapping out your inner journey, by talking about how each plot point relates to the thread of the character arc.

Also note that there's a line, in italics, that gives you the general idea of what that quarter of the story is about, with respect to the character arc.

Theme

Finally, I feel compelled to ask you, "What is the theme of your story?"

And then, "Why are you cringing?"

No, you don't have to have a theme. But sometimes they just crop up, and they're quite brilliant. So if it happens, notice it, and then keep it in mind while you're writing so it can blossom.

9. Romance Arc

In life, we are often trapped in an Identity of who we think we are.
In fiction, a character moves from that Identity to the Essence of who he was meant to be.
In romance, a pair of characters makes the transition from Identity to Essence.
This is what makes them perfect for each other
and makes lasting love possible—
the "you complete me" effect

- Why are your characters perfect for each other?
- Why do they need each other?
- What are the internal identity issues (inner demons) that will keep them apart?
- What are the external plot issues that will keep them apart?

What are the major plot points?
II-
FPP-
PP1-
MP-
PP2-
SPP-
FAS-
KO-
End-

Act 1: Intro of the orphans
Establishes all the set-up points for the story, including how the character is alone and why they need this relationship.

Opening

- What does each character lack or need and how will you show that when you introduce them?
    - Hero:
    - Shero:

Inciting Incident

- When you put these characters together, how will you hint that, at the core of their true selves or who they are*meant to be*, they are perfect for each other?
- How will you show what aspects of their personal identities, who they *think* they are, will get in the way of the relationship?

First Plot Point

- *External Relationship:* What happens at the FPP that will force the characters into each other's worlds?
- *Internal Relationship:* How will you show that the characters are attracted to each other?

Act 2: The wanderer, dazed and confused by attraction
In which the characters try to cope with feelings of attraction and desire they're not prepared to act on

Regrouping

- How do the characters react to each other immediately following the FPP as they decide what to do next?

Pinch Point 1

- What is PP1 and how does it affect the relationship?

Midpoint: The Flip

- What happens at the MP?
- *External:* How does the MP flip the story on its ear and change the context in which the romance is happening?
- *Internal:* How does the MP create a flip in terms of how one character (or both) thinks about the other?

Act 3: [redacted line from an 80s song about shooting walls, heartache, and being a warrior, because copyright]
In which the characters get together only to screw it up royally

The Doomed Plan

- What is the new plan to go for the goal and why is it doomed?

PP2: The Doomstick

- What is the wicked smackdown dealt to the characters?
- *External:* How does this cause the characters to reach a new level in the relationship?
- *Internal:* How are the characters still in their Identity and how will that lead to the Black Moment?

Black Moment

- What triggers the characters to retreat to their Identity?
- What happens at the Black Moment and how does it sever the relationship?

Dark Period

- During the dark period, how will you show that the characters long for the relationship?
    - Hero:
    - Shero:

Second Plot Point

- What is the SPP and how does it work to prove the characters want to be together?

Act 4: Victory of the Ultimate Badass Martyrs
In which the characters fully become who they're meant to be, save the day, boy gets girl and she gets him right back

Final Action Sequence

- In the FAS, how will you show the characters sacrifice their emotional armor and face their inner demons?
- How will they demonstrate their love and commitment to each other?

Climax

- At the climax, how will you show that the characters have become who they were meant to be, and how does that allow them to work together to achieve a Knock Out against their antagonistic force?
  - Hero:
  - Shero:

Denouement

- At the End, how will you show the characters in the relationship, as the people they were meant to be, and perfect for each other?

Explanation

In case you haven't seen it before, s*hero* is a modern term for *heroine.* Because the word *heroine* is often associated with damsels in distress, modern female protagonists are often called sheroes, to suggest that they can save themselves, save the day, save the world.

A lot books in the Romance genre have dual protagonists, with two points of view, giving more or less equal weight to each character. That's basically the way we'll be thinking as we walk through this sheet.

When you give your hero and shero equal angst and equal time in the spotlight, you'll want to consider them both the protagonists. They each get their own protagonist character sheet, and you work a character arc sheet for each one.

Some authors prefer to put one character in the spotlight. Even if they choose to use two points of view throughout the story, it's definitely *about* one character's journey more than the other. This works especially well in shorter novels and novellas, where you just don't have time to throw in that extra thread. In that case, you would only need to work on the character arc for your spotlight character.

Why are your characters perfect for each other?

Why do they need each other?

It may not seem like it at first, but somehow, your characters are right for each other. If readers can spot a lack in one character that matches up to something another character can provide (especially if it seems like *only* that character can provide it), they will 'ship your pairing, and 'ship it hard. (*'Ship* is a slang term used in fandom. It is a noun that means, roughly, *relationship*, and also a verb that means *to support a relationship.*)

What are the internal identity issues (inner demons) that will keep them apart? (Internal Relationship- Identity vs. Essence)

In case you're skipping around, this refers back to the sheet on Character Arc. This is the thing about them that changes, internally, from the beginning of the story to the end.

This thing may be part of what keeps your lovers apart until you're ready to put them together.

What are the external plot issues that will keep them apart?

The importance of keeping your lovers apart cannot be overemphasized.

Tension

Tension happens when we see someone need something that *can* be granted, but is, instead, withheld. They want it, and we want it for them.

Sexual tension is when the characters want each other, but hold back.

Emotional tension is when a character needs to feel something that is denied them, like love, acknowledgment, comfort, etc.

Romance novels are all about playing with tension, and the emotions of the characters and readers alike.

For this reason, it's very helpful to have good reasons to keep your characters apart. After all, we know that, ultimately, your lovers are perfect for each other. So *something* has to keep them from realizing it right away and getting together by page three.

Also, coming up with legitimate reasons, grounded in story and character, will keep you from resorting to writing a lot of bickering and misunderstandings and calling it conflict.

Major Plot Points

Yes, write them again! Same reasoning. Get them on the page, refresh your memory, see what new insights you come up with this time.

Weaving the Thread

Just like with the character arc, this is the point where you work through all the major events of the story, this time thinking about how they affect the romantic relationship.

I've used the term **Black Moment** in here. That's the point, in many Romance novels, at which the characters temporarily break up. It's often followed by a **Dark Period**, in which the characters miss each other and the relationship.

Also note that, in each act, there's a line in italics that describes what happens in this quarter of the story with respect to the romance.

10. Subplot

- What characters are involved in your subplot?
- What is the subplot about?
- Does the subplot have a goal? How does it resolve?
- How does the subplot begin? How is it introduced?
- What are the major plot points?

II-
FPP-
PP1-
MP-
PP2-
SPP-
FAS-
KO-
End-

Act 1: Intro of the Orphan

Establishes all the set-up points for the story, including what the character wants, needs, and lacks, what the character has to win or lose.

Opening

- Is there anything that needs to be planted or set up for your subplot in the first act?

Inciting Incident

- How will you introduce your subplot to the story?

First Plot Point

- What is the first turning point of your subplot? What causes the readers to engage in it?

Act 2: The Wanderer sets off

In which the character tries to learn skills and gather resources while coping with an unfamiliar world

Regrouping

- What happens in your subplot following the first plot point?
- Is there a plan of action involved in the subplot?

Pinch Point 1

- Is there an early obstacle in the subplot, or some event that occurs in the middle of act 2?
- Does PP1 of the main plot affect the subplot?

Midpoint: The Flip

- What occurs in the subplot in the middle of the story?
- Do revelations that occur in main plot affect the subplot?
- Is there a change in how the characters approach the subplot?

Act 3: The Warrior

In which the character goes on the warpath, only to be smacked down

The Doomed Plan

- Is there a new plan in the subplot?

PP2: The Doomstick

- Is there an obstacle or event in the subplot that occurs in act 3?
- Does PP2 (or the Black Moment) affect the subplot?
- Does the subplot contribute to PP2 (or the Black Moment)?

Second Plot Point

- Is there a turning point in the subplot, at the end of Act 3?
- Does the SPP of the main plot affect the subplot? Does the subplot help the characters at the SPP?

Act 4: Ultimate Badass Martyr

In which the character fully becomes who s/he was meant to be, saves the day, wins the prize.

- How is the subplot resolved?
- Does the subplot tie into the Climax?
- Does the subplot play out at the very end of the story, or before that?

Explanation

In a Romance, by the time you have two character arcs and a romance thread woven into your main plot, you don't even need a subplot. But you might have one, especially if you run a subplot to introduce a different set of characters for a subsequent book. And certainly, you may have a subplot, or more than one subplot, in other genres.

This sheet is very similar to the previous two. The first set of questions allows you to clarify your ideas about the basic elements of your subplot.

Following this, you'll list all your major plot points. Again! Remember to write them out, rather than copy/pasting them, to see what new insights you've gained from all the work you've done. Remember that you're writing the plot points of your *main plot*, not your subplot.

In the next section, you can begin to come up with the major events of your subplot. I'm treating this as if it's following along with all the bells and whistles that a main plot gets. But sometimes, subplots just *aren't that detailed.* So, if yours isn't, you may be skipping questions that don't seem to apply and that's okay.

What's not okay is to drop your subplot. So if you skip questions, try to write something else that happens in your subplot, or that relates your subplot to another story event. You want your subplot to continue to pop up every now and then, to remind the reader that there's something else going on—and so the reader doesn't worry that you forgot about it! Don't let a whole act go by without mention.

Since a subplot doesn't necessarily have the same guideposts that your main plot does, pay attention to the italicized descriptions, and see if they help you craft what happens in your subplot in each quarter.

CHAPTER 7: FLESHING THINGS OUT

More Brainstorming!

Is your brain fried yet?

Well too bad.

But these are totally optional. I made these two sheets because, while I know my story by this point, sometimes I can't get going on the day's writing because I can't think of those *things that happen* to actually write about.

Sometimes we get stuck because we can't narrow down the possibilities from the infinite. The first step to this is capturing some of that infinite and writing it down.

Sometimes we get stuck because we can't think of just the right thing that pertains the story. However, as we see in television series all the time, sometimes the important moments that move the overall narrative happen while the characters are engaged in seemingly unrelated tasks or storylines.

These exercises are just to come up with a pool of things that could happen, so that you have them available to you. When you're writing, having this available might help you stay in the story world and keep going, instead of taking time off to figure out what happens next.

You can also use these exercises to come up with material when you're trying to go from concept to premise, and at other times during the planning process.

When you're done with these, go back over your Worldbuilding and Character worksheets and add any details that have come to you while developing your story. And there will be a little more about detail in Chapter 9.

11. Event Brainstorm 1

This exercise has two parts. The first is just to write down Things That Could Happen In My Book. These are things in your story world (town, school, kingdom, haunted house, dungeon, glittering metropolis, domed colony, ranch, plantation) that would engage the attentions of your characters. Think in terms of events. Natural disasters, festivals, competitions, social gatherings, project stages, visitors… Don't worry about what you might do with these yet. This is a brainstorm, so just feel free to feel like anything could happen and jot down ideas which may become setups, scenes, or sequences of scenes in your story.

Things that could happen in my book…

12. Event Brainstorm 2

The second part of the exercise is to look at that list and think about what problems those events might cause for your characters. For those ideas that make it into the story, these problems will become the conflicts for your characters to overcome that make your scenes dynamic (as opposed to two characters discussing a problem over coffee to get information across). The problems you come up with here could give you goals that will drive your story when the main story goal feels too big, too far away, and wholly unreachable.

Look back at your list from part 1. Come up with problems inspired by those events. Look back on this exercise when you need that next thing to throw at your characters.

Problems I could give my characters…

Location Location Location

We've already done worldbuilding, but now we're going to do set design.

Earlier, we worked on some big picture inspiration for the world in which your story takes place. Now that you have a better sense of what *happens* in the story, you'll have a better sense of what locations you need to scout and what sets need to be built.

Screenwriters know where their scenes are going to take place. It says right there, in the script: INT. [Internal] DINER—DAY. All the locations are in the script so that locations can be scouted and sets can be built, before they start filming.

You don't have "people" for that. You have to research your own locations and create your own sets.

There's a danger in this, as we've talked about before, of creating more than you need, and then using details that aren't relevant. Bleh. But that's why we're going to try to build the set around what's relevant to your story.

By this time, you're getting a fair idea of the scenes that are going to take place in your story. You may add a few more, once you get to the beat sheets in the next chapter, but then you'll just come back and add any new locations later. By now, you can tell the story to another person in a *this happens, and then this happens, and then this happens* sense.

Get started on your locations by looking at the last iteration of what is shaping up to be your outline. Make a list of the scenes you can see that you need. Next to each one, write a location.

13. Locations

Like **Character: Supporting,** this is a sheet you fill out as many times as you need, then keep it in your story bible for easy reference.

- Is this an indoor or outdoor location?
- Does it have a name?
- What characters are or will be associated with this location?
- What atmosphere or feeling will you try to create in this location?
    - Use the five senses to think of some details that will convey the atmosphere you plan to create.
- How will the place make the characters feel?
- What details do you need to plant that will be relevant to the story?
- Is there a backstory involved with this location? How is that revealed?
- Is there an arrangement of the place that's important to the action?
- Are there any important props here?
- What details of the location could remind us about the story world?
- What details of the location could strengthen our understanding of the character(s)

Explanation

Making a sheet or note for each location in your story is a great thing to do for your story bible. *Especially* if you're writing a series, this can help you keep track of details, and save you tons of time looking things up to see what you already said about a place. Keep your bible handy, and add notes every time you say something new about the location. If you tend to give each new scene a read-through before moving on, try making a habit of adding to your location notes and character notes as part of that process.

- Is this an indoor or outdoor location?
- It could very well be both.
- Does it have a name?
- What characters are or will be associated with this location?

Sometimes a location will be strongly associated with a character. Josie's Bar. Pete's office. Grandma's house. If there are people who regularly inhabit the space, and if you'll use them in the story, jot down their names.

You can also write down the characters who will be brought there by the story. Your protagonist, antagonist, supporting characters.

- What atmosphere or feeling will you try to create in this location?
    - Use the five senses to think of some details that will convey the atmosphere you plan to create.

The key thing here is not the five senses, it's the *atmosphere*. What are you trying to convey about this place. Is it cheerful, chaotic, foreboding? What details can you come up with to give the reader that sense of the place?

The use of the five senses is merely to give you a way to brainstorm for details. Don't feel like you need to come up with something for each one, since using all five senses in a description, especially all at once, is often too much detail and intrusive to your narrative.

- How will the place make the characters feel?

If you describe an empty warehouse in a way that makes it seem foreboding, the character will probably feel anxious or even frightened.

But if you describe a warm and cozy parlor, and the character feels anxious or frightened, that signals the reader that something else is at work. That's intriguing.

- What details do you need to plant that will be relevant to the story?
- Is there a backstory involved with this location? How is that revealed?
- Is there an arrangement of the place that's important to the action?
- Are there any important props here?

Details like the arrangement of furniture or objects at hand are especially useful in planning out things like fight scenes. If you know an escape is going to hinge on a thug tripping over the edge of a carpet, you'll want to include the elegant, fringed carpets in your description of the room long before you need them.

- What details of the location could remind us about the story world?

For the reader, immersion in the story world comes from constant reminders. Harry Potter is a fantastic example. We are constantly reminded that magic exists and that we're in a magical place, even when the action of the scene is about something else.

- What details of the location could strengthen our understanding of the character(s)?

This might be mentioning the character's connection to the place. It might be showing us the character's reaction to the place, or to objects there. It might be that showing how the character interacts with objects there tells us something about the character we didn't know, or reinforces an important trait.

CHAPTER 8: BEATING IT OUT

What are story beats?

Story beats are all the individual actions that make up your story. This happens, then this happens, then this happens…

Right now, you've got your major things that happen, and you know how they affect and drive the story. But there are still holes to be filled.

For the four beat sheets, go through and answer the questions. Then list the beats by scene, for example:

Scene 1

Shero comes home from work. Details about the shero's life and work.

On the way to her apartment, her landlord reminds her about the rent.

Details about the shero's apartment.

Shero discovers the rent money is missing. She suspects her roommate and leaves to track her down.

This gives me, at a glance, everything I want to talk about in my first scene. (Or everything we'll see in the first scene of *Pretty Woman.*)

You may decide that you don't want to do all the beat sheets at this time. Instead, you may decide to do each beat sheet as you finish the previous quarter. That way, you're refreshing yourself on the upcoming material, and you can take into account new directions and new details that came to you in the writing.

Also note that I've included questions that pertain to writing a romance, including the use of dual protagonists. Just skip these if they don't apply.

You'll also notice that you're rewriting a lot of things you've already written down before. Because we're always revisiting, refining, expanding. And this is your final refresh before you sit down to prose your heart out.

14. Act 1 Beat Sheet

In Which The Hero Is An Orphan...

- What is the hook or question that happens within the first few scenes?
- How will you introduce the hero? What will allow the reader to connect with the hero?
- How will you introduce the shero? What will allow the reader to connect with the shero?
- When and how do the hero and shero meet?
- What is the theme of the story?
- How will you allude to the theme in Part 1?
- What events will you foreshadow and how?
- What are the hero's inner demons? How will you show that?
- What are the shero's inner demons? How will you show that?
- What's at stake for the hero? When the FPP happens what does he have to gain and lose?
- What's at stake for the shero? When the FPP happens what does she have to gain and lose?
- Are there other characters introduced in Part 1 who will continue through the story? List them, their relationships to the characters, their functions in the story.
- How does the FPP come about?
- How does the FPP unveil the antagonistic force?

List the scenes and beats of Act 1

15. Act 2 Beat Sheet

In Which The Hero is a Wanderer...

- How does the hero react to the FPP event?
- How does the shero react to the FPP event?
- What are the characters' new goals?
- What is their retreat and regrouping?
- What is their plan to take action and how is it doomed?
- What is Pinch Point 1? How does the antagonistic force take center stage in this scene?
- How are the main characters affected by PP1?
- How will you move into the Midpoint scene or sequence?
- What happens at the MP?

List scenes and beats of Act 2

16. Act 3 Beat Sheet

In Which the Hero is a Warrior

- How does the hero react to the Midpoint event? What's different now?
- How does the shero react to the Midpoint event? What's different now?
- How do the characters take proactive action?
- How are the characters fighting their inner demons? How will you show that?
- What is Pinch Point 2? How will you show the evolution of the antagonistic force?
- How do the characters react to PP2?
- Is there a Black Moment in the sense of a break-up or break down of relations between the hero and shero?
- Is there an all is lost moment where everything seems impossible for your characters? How do they react to that?
- How does the SPP come about?
- How does the SPP send your characters into Act 4?

List the scenes and beats for Act 3

17. Act 4 Beat Sheet

In Which the Hero Is the Ultimate Badass Martyr...

- What is the new plan to go after the goal?
- Is there a surprise in store? Will the plan hit a snag?
- What is the final action sequence? How do the characters get to the climax scene?
- What is the climax of the story?
- How are the characters directly responsible for the defeat of the antagonist?
- How do the characters come to terms with their inner demons? How will you show that they are no longer the people they thought the were, at the beginning of the story, and are now the people they were meant to be?
- Are there any loose ends to tie up?
- Will the characters receive any awards or praise?
- How will you show the characters as they were meant to be, enjoying their victory?What is the happily ever after moment?

List the scenes and beats of Act 4

CHAPTER 9: PREPPING TO WRITE

I'm a prepper, she's a prepper....

Wouldn't you like to be a prepper too?

You've done a lot, and that's great. Can you over-prep? Sure. You can fall into the trap of prepping as procrastination. You can do so much pre-writing work that you stifle your creativity when it comes time to actually sit down and do the writing. You should absolutely be cautious of those dangers. How much is just enough is different for everyone, and only you can answer that. So when you feel like it's time to stop, you stop. You think about what worked for you on this project, and you tweak your process for the next one.

That said, I want to talk to you about coming to work prepared.

There's a little ebook out there called 2K TO 10K: WRITING FASTER, WRITING BETTER, AND WRITING MORE OF WHAT YOU LOVE by Rachel Aaron. It's a short, inspiring read about how the author went from writing 2,000 words a day, to writing 10,000, and a lot of it is about being prepared. It's about showing up to work knowing what you're going to write, and not spending half your allotted writing time staring at a blank screen and trying to figure it out.

If you've completed the Toolkit up to this point, you're well on your way.

The ideas in this chapter are some things you can take notes on to keep you from getting stuck. They're to keep you from having to stop writing, to pull yourself out of the flow of words and your story world, in order to go figure things out or do research. Once you read through the short list I have, you'll get the idea, and should be able to come up with your own ideas which pertain to your story.

This can be important for "other" worlds, too. Some people are great at making up future technology or naming races and places on the fly. If you're not, make some up ahead, so you have them on hand.

If the idea of researching these points beforehand doesn't work for you, or if things come up in the writing that you didn't think about in the planning phase, may I humbly suggest that you learn to embrace the brackets?

Eloise knew the ensemble was terribly fetching. Her new [costume description]. It had just arrived from the dressmaker the day before, and her maid had pronounced it…

Mia pulled her gun from the drawer. It was a [gun description]that had been given to her by…

In that way, you can roll on through your work period, without abandoning your work for the Google. Remember to use more brackets for anything related, like the parts of Eloise's outfit, or the number of shots Mia's gun can fire. And remember to do a Find search at some point, to make sure you've removed all the brackets from the final document.

Timeline

You think you don't need it now, but a timeline can be such a helpful reference when you're 60,000 words into a novel and need to know something you wrote several story days ago—which you actually wrote two months ago, in real time. Having that information at your fingertips can not only save you time searching and re-reading, but also the loss of inspiration and momentum that can happen in the meantime.

Sometimes, making a general timeline of planned events before you start can help you avoid the kinds of sequence errors that make you cringe when your beta readers point them out. Additionally, making such a list can help you fill in bits of your books when you see that you can spice up a lackluster scene by setting up for something that will happen later.

This does not have to be fancy or pretty or make any sense to anyone but you.

Your "dates" can be November 4, November 11, November 27; Monday, Tuesday, Thursday; 8am, 8:30am, 10am; 1945, 1952, 1964... When you don't want to fix a specific date, try labels like Day 1 for the first day of your story and go from there. I have a series timeline where the beginning of the first story is Year 1, anything before that goes into the negative, and anything after counts up from that first story. My books usually start as Day 1, and then I go back and add days of the week once I get some fixed points of reference (okay, I know this is on a Saturday night, so two days ago when that happened must have been Thursday).

The nice thing about making your timeline as a list in Evernote (or any computery thing) is that you can add new entries between old ones without tearing holes in your page with an eraser. And, when you mention an event you have notes about, you can link to those notes.

Sometimes (often) plans differ from what actually comes out in the writing. Make a point of coming back to update the timeline whenever you write an event of sequence.

If you're a visual person, feel free to draw out your timeline on a sheet of paper you can tape above your workspace. Snap a picture of it and save it in Evernote, just in case it becomes a victim of a preschooler's graffiti or a meme-induced hilarity beverage spew.

Scene, Cast, and Location Lists

Proposed Scene List

You might decide you want to make a nice, clean scene list, free of the clutter of your beat sheet. Of course, some might call this an ***outline***… It can be nice to have a list where you can zero in on the few lines that represent Today's Assignment, and then get going.

Finished Scene List

Sometimes things don't go the way you planned, and sometimes it's hard to keep track of what you did vs. what you meant to do. You might decide you want to keep a list of scenes you've finished, with a short description of what happened, and any important points you need to keep track of. Like an outline, this will help you see your finished story so far, at a glance.

Cast List

This is, simply, a list of your characters, especially useful if you have a series and/or large cast.

If you keep your notes on paper, you might just want to keep the list to remind you of a few, key details about each character.

If you organize in a program like Evernote, you can create an index that contains individual links to your detailed notes, so that you can look things up, quickly and painlessly, when you're plotting, writing, or updating your bible.

Location List

Same logic applies here, as to the cast list.

Costumes, Props, and other Tidbits

Special Costumes

This may not be a thing in your story, but if you have special costume needs, maybe you want think about that, have notes ready for that, before you get there.

If you have a special event, what is everyone wearing?

Do you need to research armor?

Do you need to research period dress?

Do you need a harness for your mountain climber scene or…ahem…other adventure?

Fashion and Brand Names

Some characteristics of people and places benefit by talking about designer labels. What kind of suit is he wearing? Watch? Shoes? What about her shoes? Bag? Scarf?

If you're using designer labels as shorthand to communicate something to the reader about your characters or their world, you might want to do a little online shopping and have some ideas on hand.

Weapons

Will weapons appear in your story? Will you talk about them in a generic sense, or specifics? Is there anything you need to know about how to use the weapon, or about its effects?

Procedural

Do you have a medical issue or emergency?

Will your character interact with (or as) law enforcement?

Is there a technical process that takes place in the story?

Is there an event for which societal protocol must be followed?

If there are issues or procedures you're not comfortable writing about now, chances are you're still not going to know about them when the character is living those moments.

Past Events

Your character has a backstory, but does anything else in your story have relevant history?

Was there a past event in the town that matters? What happened? What was involved? Who was affected? When was it? Was it resolved? How?

Did something happen in the business the character works for that will be relevant? What are the details? Who knows about it? How does it affect the story?

Was there a historical event you'll need to talk about? A law that was passed? A battle fought? What were the dates? What details do you need to relate to the reader?

Name Lists

You can also make short lists of names for extra characters who show up on set, or for places like businesses or other towns that might be mentioned.

If you can be trusted to work with a browser open (without wandering off to Facebook or Gmail), you can make a list of helpful online name generators and other types of generators to give you quick fixes to these problems.

If you tend to write the same kinds of stories over and over, maintaining your own list, where you're able to cross off names you've used, might serve you better.

Schedule It

If you're enjoying the idea of the Toolkit, maybe you love making lists. *I* love making lists.

I recently read an article that to-do lists aren't nearly as effective as they could be, if the lister doesn't *prioritize* and *schedule* the items on the list. It made a lot of sense. We don't always think of things in the order in which they should be done.

With the Toolkit, there's definitely some leeway as far as order. You may need to work more on your character before you can figure out your story. You may need to jump ahead to thinking about your romance before you can really commit to conflict. And certainly, as you go along, you're going to go back and revisit parts of the planning as new and better ideas occur to you.

Still, it gives you a process to work through. It brings order to the chaos of making your story out of the infinite possibilities available. Because it's broken down into discrete sections, it's easy to put those sections on a calendar. *Plan your work, work your plan.*

Stop saying someday, and say what day. (Today is good.)

And remember—it's *your* calendar. Those of us who are perfectionists sometimes have problems making that kind of commitment (or any commitment) for fear of not meeting it. Let's work on that, for our own good. If you need more time, if you need to bump something back or change the order, that's *okay.*

Thank You and Good Luck

Sincerely, thank you for purchasing Story Toolkit, and for investing your time in reading these ideas.. I hope you learned something you didn't know, or saw something organized in a way that made you go—ah-ha!

Most of all, I hope you can't wait to sit down and create a story. I hope you delight in the planning. I hope you fall so hard into the writing zone, into your story world, that every time you sit down to write you walk around the real world in a daze afterward. (And I hope you drive safely while that happens.)

I hope you absolutely astonish yourself with your own creation.

Blank Worksheets

0. Novel Checklist

1. Initial Concept
2. Worldbuilding
3. Antagonist, Main Conflict, and Stakes
4. Major Plot Points
5. Character: Protagonist
6. Character: Antagonist
7. Character: Supporting (one for each)
8. Character Arc
9. Romance Arc
10. Subplot
11. Event Brainstorm 1
12. Event Brainstorm 2
13. Locations (one for each)
14. Act 1 Beat Sheet
15. Act 2 Beat Sheet
16. Act 3 Beat Sheet
17. Act 4 Beat Sheet
18. Timeline
19. Proposed Scene List
20. Finished Scene List
21. Cast List
22. Location List

....and any special lists you may add, links to research, etc.

1. Initial Concept

- What is the beginning concept or inspiration for this story?

- What do you know about the main characters? List some wants/needs and fears.

- What do you know about the story world?

- What do you know about the story problem? What is the main character's goal, motivation, and conflict?

- What do you know about the antagonist?

2. Worldbuilding 1/3

A lot of this is for inspiration purposes. Do not feel that you need to answer all the questions. Don't force what's not relevant.

- **When?**
    - Time period- (Current day, historic period, future, alternate reality…)
    - Jot down some things you know about the time period in which your story takes place and how that will affect the story and/or characters.
    - Season-
    - How does the season affect the story? Holidays?
    - Weather conditions that affect the story?
- **Where?**
    - Where does your story take place? (Town, country, planet, school…)
    - Jot down a general idea of how the world itself will affect the story and its characters.
    - Geography
        - Any mountains, bodies of water, roads, lack of roads, borders, flora, fauna, etc., that will affect the story

Worldbuilding 2/3

- **Who?**
  - Are there specific groups of people in your world that will influence the story?
  - Ethnic cultures
  - Cliques or organizations
  - Powerful families or clans
  - Societal rules or norms, culture

Worldbuiilding 3/3

- **What?**
  - **Politics?**
    - Are there details about the government or political situation that affect the story?
    - Are there economic details that affect the story?
    - Is there or has there been a war that affects the story?
  - **Technology?**
  - **History?**
    - Regional history, ethnic heritage

3. Antagonist, Main Conflict, and Stakes 1/2

Part 1

- Conflict or Villain? Where do you start?

You start where you're inspired to start. Write whatever you can about either the conflict or the villain in your story.

Part 2

- If you wrote about the conflict, write about the antagonist who would confront your character(s) with it.

- If you wrote about a villain, write down a problem he could cause for your hero.

3. Antagonist, Main Conflict, and Stakes, 2/2

Part 3

Let's take our thinking a little deeper...

- What is your protagonist's weakness?
- Why is your antagonist the one perfect agent to exploit that weakness and force the protagonist to overcome it?
- In what way(s) are your protagonist and antagonist alike?

Part 4

Let's talk stakes. Consequences.

Assumption: at the end of the novel, your protagonist solves the story problem. Protagonist "wins," antagonist "loses."

- What does your protagonist gain by solving the story problem and being the winner?
- If your antagonist were to win at the end of the story, what would he gain?
- What does your antagonist lose at the end of the story?
- If your protagonist were to fail, what would he lose?

4. Major Plot Points 1/3

Story = A CHARACTER pursues a GOAL because of MOTIVATION, but is hampered by CONFLICT.

Character
Who is your protagonist?

Goal
What is the ultimate end goal for your protagonist?

Motivation
Why is your protagonist in pursuit of his goal?

Conflict
What is the antagonist (or antagonistic force) that stands between your protagonist and his goal?

How/why does the antagonist attempt to prevent the protagonist from attaining or achieving his goal?

4. Major Plot Points 2/3

To chart the course of a journey, one must know one's destination.
In a story, we like to call that
The End.

Climax

- What do you know about the climax of the story?

- How does the ending deliver a knock-out experience?

- How does the ending solve the story problem?

- How is the protagonist the catalyst for solving the story problem?

4. Major Plot Points 3/3

***No one shows up at the deli and says,
"Give me anything on rye."
What's in the middle is pretty important.***

Brainstorm for ideas about the major events of your story. Refer back to the book to refresh your memory on the functions of these plot points. It's okay to be vague on what you don't know, but write something, even if it's just a reminder of what needs to happen functionally at that point in the story. Remember, this isn't an outline, we're still just brainstorming.

Act 1
II-

FPP-

Act 2
PP1-

MP-

Act 3
PP2-

SPP-

Act 4
KO-

END-

5. Character: Protagonist 1/4

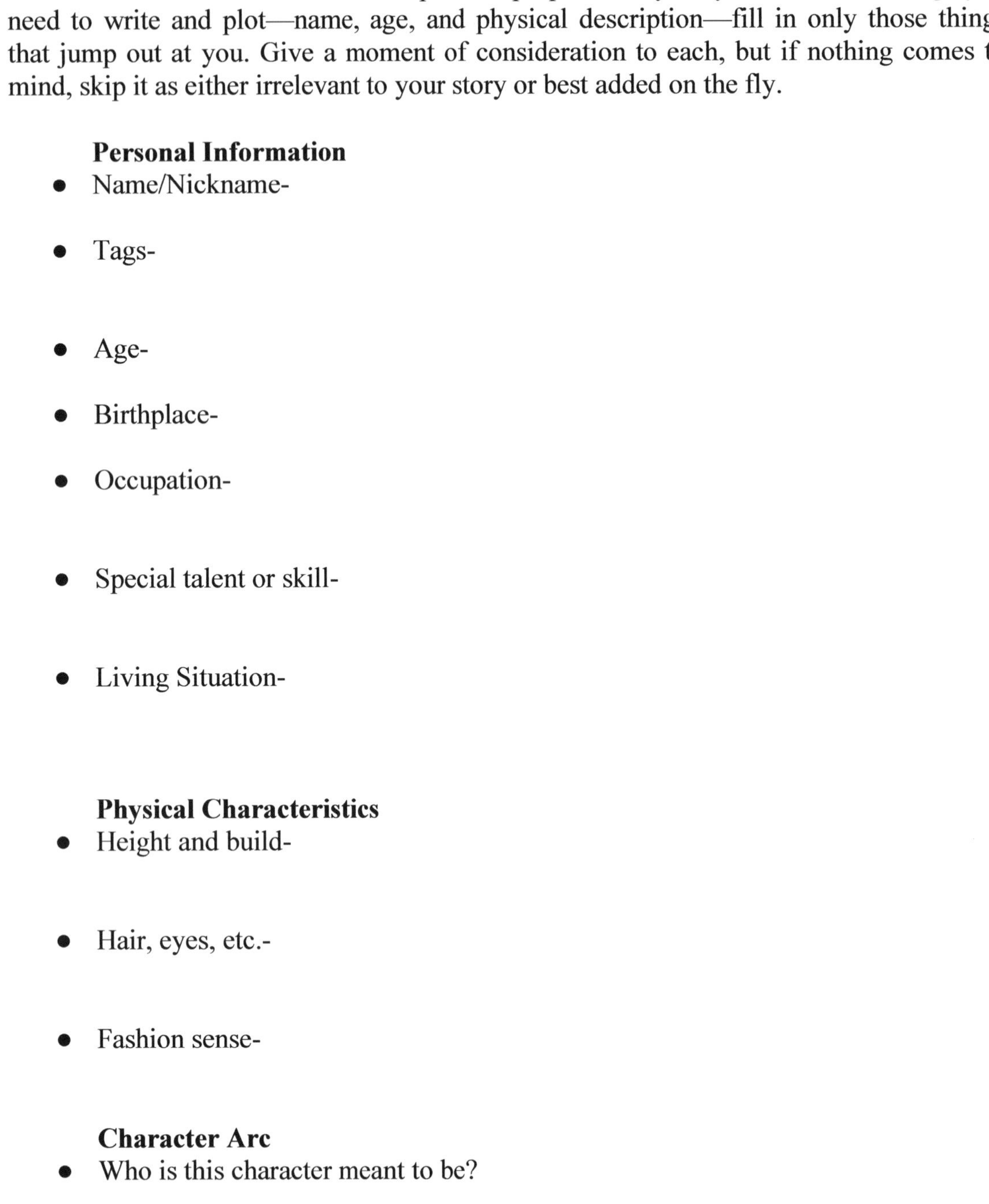

The bulk of this list is for inspiration purposes only. Beyond the basic things you need to write and plot—name, age, and physical description—fill in only those things that jump out at you. Give a moment of consideration to each, but if nothing comes to mind, skip it as either irrelevant to your story or best added on the fly.

Personal Information

- Name/Nickname-
- Tags-
- Age-
- Birthplace-
- Occupation-
- Special talent or skill-
- Living Situation-

Physical Characteristics

- Height and build-
- Hair, eyes, etc.-
- Fashion sense-

Character Arc

- Who is this character meant to be?
- How is that different from who they think they are when the story begins?

5. Character: Protagonist 2/4

Relationships

- List any relevant people and their relationship with, or affect on, the character. Parents, siblings, best friend, worst enemy, boss...

5. Character: Protagonist 3/4

Dear Things

- What does your character really care about?

Personality Style

- Response to change (hates it? seeks it? rolls with it?)-
- Coping methods-
- Best quality-
- Worst flaw-
- What does this character think is the worst thing that could happen to them?

Favorite Things

- Color-
- Music-
- Place (why?)-
- Time of day-
- Holiday or season-
- Food-
- Activity/Hobby-
- Aversions-

5. Character: Protagonist 4/4

Defining Moments

- What is the worst thing that has ever happened to this character?
- What is this character's favorite memory?
- Was there a moment from the past that continues to affect the character today?

Survival and Attitude

- What does the character always carry?
- What does the character always have in the refrigerator (in their living space, etc.)?

Relevant Backstory

- What about this character's past is relevant to the story?

Likability

- Why do you/why will we love this character?

6. Character: Antagonist 1/5

The bulk of this list is for inspiration purposes only. Beyond the basic things you need to write and plot—name, age, and physical description—fill in only those things that jump out at you. Give a moment of consideration to each, but if nothing comes to mind, skip it as either irrelevant to your story or best added on the fly.

Personal Information

- Name/Nickname-
- Tags-
- Age-
- Birthplace-
- Occupation-
- Special talent or skill-
- Living Situation-

Physical Characteristics

- Height and build-
- Hair, eyes, etc.-
- Fashion sense-

6. Character: Antagonist 2/5

Character Arc

- Who is this character meant to be?

- How is that different from who they think they are when the story begins?

- Why will we love to hate this character?

Relationships

- List any relevant people and their relationship with, or affect on, the character. Parents, siblings, best friend, worst enemy, boss...

6. Character: Antagonist 3/5

Dear Things

- What does your character really care about?

Bad Guy Stuff

- Why is this character at odds with your protagonist?
- Why is this character perfect for exploiting the weakness of your protagonist?
- Is your antagonist genuinely bad or just misunderstood? How did that happen?
- What does this character think about himself?
- Could this character be redeemed?

Personality Style

- Response to change (hates it? seeks it? rolls with it?)-
- Coping methods-
- Best quality-
- Worst flaw-
- What does this character think is the worst thing that could happen to them?

6. Character: Antagonist 4/5

Favorite Things

- Color-
- Music-
- Place (why?)-
- Time of day-
- Holiday or season-
- Food-
- Activity/Hobby-
- Aversions-

Defining Moments

- What is the worst thing that has ever happened to this character?
- What is this character's favorite memory?
- Was there a moment from the past that continues to affect the character today?
- What started your antagonist down the wrong path?

6. Character: Antagonist 5/5

Survival and Attitude

- What does the character always carry?

- What does the character always have in the refrigerator (in their living space, etc.)?

Relevant Backstory

- What about this character's past is relevant to the story?

Reader Response

- Why will we love to hate this character?

7. Character: Supporting 1/2

1. Make one for each character.
2. Keep these simple. Leave these characters open to be what you need them to be, in order tofacilitatethe writing.
3. Tag with character name, book title, series name, and "bible"
4. Come back and add details as you write the story.
5. Thank yourself later.

Name

Tags

Age

Physical description

Relationship to/with main character(s)

Style

Occupation/Special skills

Is this character associated with a specific location?

Quirk

7. Character: Supporting 2/2

Likes

Hates

Fears

Living situation

Family

Relevant backstory

What does the future hold for this character?

8. Character Arc 1/7

In life, we are often trapped in an Identity of who we think we are.

In fiction, a character moves from that Identity to the Essence of who he was meant to be.

- What does your character need and lack?
- What lesson does your character need to learn?
- What does your character really care about?
- What are the internal identity issues (inner demons or skewed world view) that keep your character from attaining what they need?
- How does who he thinks he is different from who he was meant to be?
- What external plot issues will be affected by these identity issues?

8. Character Arc 2/7

What are the major plot points?

II-

FPP-

PP1-

MP-

PP2-

SPP-

FAS-

KO-

End-

8. Character Arc 3/7

Act 1: Intro of the Orphan

Establishes all the set-up points for the story, including what the character wants, needs, and lacks, what the character has to win or lose.

Opening

- What does the character lack or need and how will you show that when you introduce them?

Inciting Incident

- What is the inciting incident? How does it begin to set up for the first plot point?

- How does the inciting incident poke at your character's fears and insecurities?

- How will you show what's at stake, what will be on the table to gain and lose at the first plot point?

- How will you show what aspects of personal identity, who they *think* they are, will get in the way of achieving the goal that will be set at the first plot point?

8. Character Arc 4/7

First Plot Point

- What is the FPP? What goal does it set for the character?

- *External Arc:* What happens at the FPP that will force the character into the story world?

- *Internal Arc:* How will you show that the character is reluctant to move forward but chooses to anyway?

8. Character Arc 5/7

Act 2: The Wanderer sets off

In which the character tries to learn skills and gather resources while coping with an unfamiliar world

Regrouping

- How does the character react immediately following the FPP? What does he decide to do next?

Pinch Point 1

- What is PP1? How does it show that the character doesn't have what it takes to stand up to the antagonistic force and achieve the goal?

Midpoint: The Flip

- What happens at the MP?

External: How does the MP flip the story on its ear and change the context?

Internal: How does the MP create a flip in terms of turning the Wanderer into a Warrior, reactive to proactive?

8. Character Arc 6/7

Act 3: The Warrior
In which the character goes on the warpath, only to be smacked down
The Doomed Plan

- What is the new plan to go for the goal and why is it doomed? (Hint: it's because of *Identity*--the character's skewed world view or inner demon that causes them to make wrong choices.)

PP2: The Doomstick

- What is the wicked smackdown dealt to the character?

- *External:* How does make it seem like *all is lost*and attainment of the goal is now impossible?

- *Internal:* How does PP2 show the character's retreat to their*Identity,* and how he is no matchfor the antagonistic force?

Second Plot Point

What is the SPP and how does it work to push the character into the final Act? What piece of the puzzle does it give the character that he didn't have before?

8. Character Arc 7/7

Act 4: Ultimate Badass Martyr

In which the character fully becomes who he was meant to be, saves the day, wins the prize.

Final Action Sequence

- In the FAS, how will you show the character facing his inner demon/learning his lesson?

Climax

- At the climax, how does the character show that he has learned his lesson and/or become who he was meant to be, and how does that allow him to finally achieve a Knock Out against the antagonistic force?

Denouement

At the End, how will you show the character has become who was meant to be?

What is the theme of your story?

9. Romance Arc 1/7

In life, we are often trapped in anIdentityofwho we think we are.

In fiction, a character moves from that Identity to theEssenceofwho s/he was meant to be.

In romance, a pair of characters makes the transition from Identity to Essence
This is what makes themperfect for each other
and makes lasting love possible--

the "you complete me" effect

- Why are your characters perfect for each other?

- Why do they need each other?

- What are the internal identity issues (inner demons) that will keep them apart?

- What are the external plot issues that will keep them apart?

9. Romance Arc 2/7

What are the major plot points?

II-

FPP-

PP1-

MP-

PP2-

SPP-

FAS-

KO-

End-

9. Romance Arc 3/7

Act 1: Intro of the orphans

Establishes all the set-up points for the story, including how the character is alone and why they need this relationship.

Opening

What does each character lack or need and how will you show that when you introduce them?

Hero:

Shero:

Inciting Incident

When you put these characters together, how will you hint that, at the core of their true selves or who they are*meant to be*, they are perfect for each other?

How will you show what aspects of their personal identities, who they *think* they are, will get in the way of the relationship?

First Plot Point

External Relationship: What happens at the FPP that will force the characters into each other's worlds?

Internal Relationship: How will you show that the characters are attracted to each other?

9. Romance Arc 4/7

Act 2: The wanderer, dazed and confused by attraction

In which the characters try to cope with feelings of attraction and desire they're not prepared to act on

Regrouping

How do the characters react to each other immediately following the FPP as they decide what to do next?

Pinch Point 1

What is PP1 and how does it affect the relationship?

Midpoint: The Flip

What happens at the MP?

External: How does the MP flip the story on its ear and change the context in which the romance is happening?

Internal: How does the MP create a flip in terms of how one character (or both) thinks about the other?

9. Romance Arc 5/7

Act 3: [redacted line from an 80s song about shooting walls, heartache, and being a warrior, because copyright]

In which the characters get together only to screw it up royally

The Doomed Plan

What is the new plan to go for the goal and why is it doomed?

PP2: The Doomstick

What is the wicked smackdown dealt to the characters?

External: How does this cause the characters to reach a new level in the relationship?

Internal: How are the characters still in their Identity and how will that lead to the Black Moment?

9. Romance Arc 6/7

Black Moment

What triggers the characters' to retreat to their Identity?

What happens at the Black Moment and how does it sever the relationship?

Dark Period

During the dark period, how will you show that the characters long for the relationship?

Hero:

Shero:

Second Plot Point

What is the SPP and how does it work to prove the characters want to be together?

9. Romance Arc 7/7

Act 4: Victory of the Ultimate Badass Martyrs

In which the characters fully become who they're meant to be, save the day, boy gets girl and she gets him right back

Final Action Sequence

In the FAS, how will you show the characters sacrifice their emotional armor and face their inner demons?

How will they demonstrate their love and commitment to each other?

Climax

At the climax, how will you show that the characters have become who they were meant to be, and how does that allow them to work together to achieve a Knock Out against their antagonistic force?

Hero:

Shero:

Denouement

At the End, how will you show the characters in the relationship, as the people they were meant to be, and perfect for each other?

10. Subplot 1/7

- What characters are involved in your subplot?

- What is the subplot about?

- Does the subplot have a goal? How does it resolve?

- How does the subplot begin? How is it introduced?

10. Subplot 2/7

What are the major plot points?

II-

FPP-

PP1-

MP-

PP2-

SPP-

FAS-

KO-

End-

10. Subplot 3/7

Act 1: Intro of the Orphan

Establishes all the set-up points for the story, including what the character wants, needs, and lacks, what the character has to win or lose.

Opening

Is there anything that needs to be planted or set up for your subplot in the first act?

Inciting Incident

How will you introduce your subplot to the story?

First Plot Point

What is the first turning point of your subplot?

What causes the readers to engage with it?

10. Subplot 4/7

Act 2: The Wanderer sets off

In which the character tries to learn skills and gather resources while coping with an unfamiliar world

Regrouping

What happens in your subplot following the first plot point?

Is there a plan of action involved in the subplot?

Pinch Point 1

Is there an early obstacle in the subplot, or some event that occurs in the middle of act 2?

Does PP1 of the main plot affect the subplot?

Midpoint: The Flip

What occurs in the subplot in the middle of the story?

Do revelations that occur in main plot affect the subplot?

Is there a change in how the characters approach the subplot?

10. Subplot 5/7

Act 3: The Warrior
In which the character goes on the warpath, only to be smacked down
The Doomed Plan
Is there a new plan in the subplot?

PP2: The Doomstick
Is there an obstacle or event in the subplot that occurs in act 3?

Does PP2 (or the Black Moment) affect the subplot?

Does the subplot contribute to PP2 (or the Black Moment)?

10. Subplot 6/7

Second Plot Point

Is there a turning point in the subplot, at the end of act 3?

Does the SPP of the main plot affect the subplot?

Does the subplot help the characters at the SPP?

10. Subplot 7/7

Act 4: Ultimate Badass Martyr

In which the character fully becomes who s/he was meant to be, saves the day, wins the prize.

How is the subplot resolved?

Does the subplot tie into the Climax?

Does the subplot play out at the very end of the story, or before that?

11. Event Brainstorm 1

Things that could happen in my book…

12. Event Brainstorm 2

Problems I could give my characters…

13. Locations 1/2

Like **Character: Supporting**, this is a sheet you fill out as many times as you need, then keep it in your story bible for easy reference.

- Is this an indoor or outdoor location?

- Does it have a name?

- What characters are or will be associated with this location?

- What atmosphere or feeling will you try to create in this location?

- Use the five senses to think of some details that will convey the atmosphere you plan to create.

13. Locations 2/2

- How will the place make the characters feel?

- What details do you need to plant that will be relevant to the story?

- Is there a backstory involved in with this location? How is that revealed?

- Is there an arrangement of the place that's important to the action?

- Are there any important props here?

- What details of the location could remind us about the story world?

- What details of the location could strengthen our understanding of the character(s)?

14. Act 1 Beat Sheet 1/3

In Which The Hero Is An Orphan...

- What is the hook or question that happens within the first few scenes?
- How will you introduce the hero? What will allow the reader to connect with the hero?
- How will you introduce the shero? What will allow the reader to connect with the shero?
- When and how do the hero and shero meet?
- What is the theme of the story?
- How will you allude to the theme in Part 1?
- What events will you foreshadow and how?

14. Act 1 Beat Sheet 2/3

- What are the hero's inner demons? How will you show that?

- What are the shero's inner demons? How will you show that?

- What's at stake for the hero? When the FPP happens what does he have to gain and lose?

- What's at stake for the shero? When the FPP happens what does she have to gain and lose?

- Are there other characters introduced in Part 1 who will continue through the story? List them, their relationships to the characters, their functions in the story.

- How does the FPP come about?

- How does the FPP unveil the antagonistic force?

14. Act 1 Beat Sheet 3/3

List the scenes and beats of Act 1

15. Act 2 Beat Sheet 1/3

In Which The Hero is a Wanderer...

- How does the hero react to the FPP event?

- How does the shero react to the FPP event?

- What are the characters' new goals?

- What is their retreat and regrouping?

- What is their plan to take action and how is it doomed?

15. Act 2 Beat Sheet 2/3

- What is Pinch Point 1? How does the antagonistic force take center stage in this scene?

- How are the main characters affected by PP1?

- How will you move into the Midpoint scene or sequence?

- What happens at the MP?

15. Act 2 Beat Sheet 3/3

List scenes and beats of Act 2

16. Act 3 Beat Sheet 1/3

In Which the Hero is a Warrior

- How does the hero react to the Midpoint event? What's different now?

- How does the shero react to the Midpoint event? What's different now?

- How do the characters take proactive action?

- How are the characters fighting their inner demons? How will you show that?

16. Act 3 Beat Sheet 2/3

- What is Pinch Point 2? How will you show the evolution of the antagonistic force?

- How do the characters react to PP2?

- Is there a Black Moment in the sense of a break-up or break down of relations between the hero and shero?

- Is there an all is lost moment where everything seems impossible for your characters? How do they react to that?

- How does the SPP come about?

- How does the SPP send your characters into Act 4?

16. Act 3 Beat Sheet 3/3

List scenes and beats for Act 3

17. Act 4 Beat Sheet 1/3

In Which the Hero Is the Ultimate Badass Martyr...

- What is the new plan to go after the goal?

- Is there a surprise in store? Will the plan hit a snag?

- What is the final action sequence? How do the characters get to the climax scene?

- What is the climax of the story?

17. Act 4 Beat Sheet 2/3

- How are the characters directly responsible for the defeat of the antagonist?

- How do the characters come to terms with their inner demons? How will you show that they are no longer the people they thought the were, at the beginning of the story, and are now the people they were meant to be?

- Are there any loose ends to tie up?

- Will the characters receive any awards or praise?

- How will you show the characters as they were meant to be, enjoying their victory?What is the happily ever after moment?

17. Act 4 Beat Sheet 3/3

List the scenes and beats of Act 4

Timeline

Proposed Scene List

For quick reference, list the scenes you plan to write, with any key points you need to remember.

Finished Scene List

Map your story as you go by writing a quick summary of each scene you finish.

Cast List

For quick reference, make a list of all the cast members in your story, an jot down any details you need to remember.

Location List

Make a list of all the locations in your story, with any key details you need to remember.

Special Lists

Make lists of things like special costumes, fashion and brand names, weapons, procedures, past events, names, etc.

Made in the USA
Middletown, DE
19 November 2019